Sweet Lorain

BOOKS BY BRUCE WEIGL

Poetry

Executioner (1976)
Like a Sackful of Old Quarrels (1977)
A Romance (1979)
The Monkey Wars (1984)
Song of Napalm (1988)
What Saves Us (1992)
Lies, Grace & Redemption (selected poems and an interview,
  edited by Harry Humes; 1995)

Translation

Poems from Captured Documents (translated from the
Vietnamese with Thanh Nguyen; 1994)

Criticism

The Giver of Morning: On Dave Smith (1983)
The Imagination as Glory: The Poetry of James Dickey
  (with T. R. Hummer; 1984)

Sweet Lorain

Bruce Weigl

TRIQUARTERLY BOOKS
NORTHWESTERN UNIVERSITY PRESS

EVANSTON, ILLINOIS

TriQuarterly Books
Northwestern University Press
Evanston, Illinois 60208-4210

Copyright © 1996 by Bruce Weigl
First published 1996
All rights reserved
Printed in the United States of America

Library of Congress Cataloging-in-Publication Data

Weigl, Bruce, 1949–
    Sweet Lorain / Bruce Weigl.
       p. cm.
    ISBN 0-8101-5053-0 (cloth). — ISBN 0-8101-5054-9 (paper).
      1. Vietnamese Conflict, 1961–1975—Ohio—Lorain—Influence—
Poetry. 2. Working class—Ohio—Lorain—Poetry. 3. Family—Ohio—
Lorain—Poetry. I. Title.
PS3573.E3835S93 1996
811'.54—dc20   95-52866
                                                        CIP

for Bill, Hank, Patrick, Pete, and Rab
(GFA forever)

Contents

Acknowledgments

I am grateful for the support of the editors of the following publications where these poems first appeared:

American Poetry Review: "Care," "Sitting with the Buddhist Monks, Hue, 1967," "Cleaning out the Shaker Gears, Elyria Foundry, Elyria, Ohio, 1971," "Elegy for Peter," "The One," "Conversation of Our Blood," "Our 17th Street Years," "At the Confluence of Memory and Desire in Lorain, Ohio," "Red Squirrel," "Brother Crow of Pearl Avenue," "Carp," "For the Novice of Tran Quoc Pagoda," "First Letter to Calumpang," and "Yes to the Voices of Eons Ago."

Antaeus: "From the House on Nguyen Du."

The New York Times: "Three Fish."

Ploughshares: "On the Ambiguity of Injury and Pain" and "Bear Meadows."

Poetry New York: "Rhapsody" and "Meditation in Hue."

Prairie Schooner: "Chain" and "Words Like Cold Whiskey between Us and Pain."

Southern Review: "That Finished Feeling."

TriQuarterly: "What I Saw and Did in the Alley," "Three Meditations at Nguyen Du," "Fever Dream in Hanoi," "Words for the Husky Girl," "My Early Training," "At the Dreamland Theater, 1959," "Seeking the Redwing," "Hymn of My Republic," and "Hanoi, Christmas 1992."

Willow Springs: "Meditation at Melville Ave." and "Meditation at La Grange" (as "Rib").

"The One" also appeared in *The Best American Poetry 1994*, edited by A. R. Ammons and David Lehman (Macmillan, 1994). "Meditation in Hue" (in a radically different version) also appeared in a special issue of *The Journal of Popular Culture*.

Many of these poems also appeared in *Van Nghe* (Hanoi), translated into Vietnamese by Nguyen Quang Thieu, editor of that journal's international literary pages.

Early drafts of some of these poems were written during two recent visits to Hanoi, during which time I had the generous support of Chinh Hu and Vu Tu Nam, co-chairs of the Vietnamese Writers' Association, and its members. My thanks also go to Dao Kim Hoa, Huu Thinh, Pham Tien Duat, Le Luu, Le Chinh, Le Hanh Le, Nguyen Quang Thieu, Hoang Yen, and in memory of Ngo Vinh Vien, among other friends in Hanoi, and to Larry Heinemann, Tim O'Brien, George Evans, Yusef Kumanyaka, Wayne Karlin, and Kevin Bowen for their brotherhood, to Toby Thompson for his council and friendship, to Denise Levertov for the inspiration of her work and her many other kindnesses, and to Gloria Emerson (for saying "Lorain! Lorain!"). I am also grateful for the support of my family. As always, thanks to RG, who enables.

Sitting with the Buddhist Monks, Hue, 1967

Cool spring air through the window,
birds waking rain in the white
limbs of the shaken birch,
I remember
I was led through an ancient
musty maze of alleyways
and rooms where people looked up
from their cooking
and their endless ledgers
as if I were a mean and clumsy spirit
lost among them.

Into darkness I was delivered,
only candlelight
to show the heads bowed
to the clasped hands
rocking in prayer.

I thought he was taking me to his whore.
They did not teach us
the words for prayer or for peace.
I'd watched his hands
gesture in the half-lit alleyway
and his hands told me to follow,
his eyes asked me for money.

I have tried to let the green war go,
but those monks looked at me

1

across their circle of knowing
and my body somehow
rose off the floor,
their voices
ringing in my skull
like the cry of gut wound
in razor grass.

I was only a boy.
I didn't want to remember.
I wanted only the lily
to keep opening.

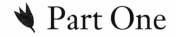 # Part One

¡*Con la belleza no se come!*
¿*Qué piensas que en la vida?*

The One

To the long mill's shadow
and stink we shared
with drunks who pissed
on the heater of our common
john
I go back.
To the bedroom I shared with my sister,
my bed squeezed
tight against the cool wall
so I could hold my body there
hot nights in the mill noise
until my legs stiffened
and I felt that hum.

In the corner of that room
waits the word
and the sound
of the belt.
My tall father
thin and muscled from mill work,
his hair black
thick and curly,
and his smile,
when he swung down on me,
I could not resist.
Through dark the belt
flashed across my back
though I knew he beat me
out of love

as when he finished
I knew to climb
inside the darkness of my own arms.
I knew the world
would stop spinning
uncontrollably
and the convulsions
stop rippling
and my mother
would come to touch me
with such care
as if I were teetering
at the edge of the abyss
and she would lead me
back into my life,
her fingers
whispering in my hair
that it would be all right,

and later still, after beer,
after the moon had risen
to its proper place
and the night
could allow some forgiveness,
he would call me into his lap,
and tell me I was the one.

What I Saw and Did in the Alley

Some lonely boy from the neighborhood
with the Saint Vitus' Dance
from when a truck
backed over his wagon
nearly crushing his skull
made a crossbow
from the leaf-springs of a car
and haunted the summer dusk streets
beyond the long mill.

I found the cat
dead in the alley,
a homemade arrow
nicely through its skull.
Running home late,
I stumbled on the cat
and had to stop.
By the scruff of his alley neck
I held Mr. unknown cat
and looked into his eyes
green as new bamboo

and reckoned our kinship
of killing
in that alley and beyond
where needful of love, and of blood
I had stunned the brown sparrow,
the robin and wren,
the wild canary in spring.

Don't ask how they felt
in my hands, still warm,
bubble of blood on their beaks;
to nowhere their dead wings unfold.

Yes to the Voices of Eons Ago

Back then I loved a spirit
who sang strange songs to me.
Across the sunlit winter square
I watched her walk on out of sight,
into the snowy branches there,
into that dubious, cold morning light.

I knew I should not look at her,
but turn my head away as if
in pleasure, and watch the storm blow in
through the square its torn clouds.
Mad sky is how it came to me;
I felt an ancient ache inside.
I knew I should have closed my eyes.
Mad sky is how it came to me.

Care

I didn't know what they wanted.
Six or seven
and in the care of two teenage
cousins drunk on beer
who dragged me through dark woods
behind their house.
I thought I saw black wings swoop down
to lift me, but no one came
so I followed them into a clearing
where they finished their beer
and loaded the rifle.
In the snow I was cold.
I watched them make a pyramid of cans
they blasted in turns with the rifle
so it sounded like someone's
bones being broken,
and then they looked at me.
They put a can in my hand
extended as far from my body
as all my strength allowed. . . .

For a long time afterwards
I felt out of sync.
In school I would fall
into tunnels of snow
in my brain towards some center
until I heard my name
called from a great distance
and felt the teacher

shake my shoulders.
That night with my cousins
drunkenly loading their rifle,
I learned that fear has a shape
and a taste in your mouth
not like metal,
but more human and wrong.
I wanted to drop my arms and run away,
but they were wildly drunk
and stumbled in the frozen snow,
the rifle tangled between them
so I was afraid to move
until a shot caught the can in my hand
on its rim
so it vibrated through my fingers,
shook my brain and then exploded
into the moonlit snow behind me.
They laughed and slapped my back,
and just as thoughtlessly
as we had descended,
we rose again into the trees
towards the warm house
and its emerald
jungle of our lives.

At the Confluence of Memory and Desire in Lorain, Ohio

Love could be a shape that unfolds
in rooms sullen and deformed by rain

Oh clothes torn off in that
frenzy

Oh seeing-eye
tongues

Oh saintly lies whispered
in evening's wrong light

Slam of hips
and her breasts would sway

I taste the bloody slit
in the night's cloth

Three Meditations at Nguyen Du

i

I have loved more than a few good men
who were boys in the green
slanting rain of bullets
cut through yellow bamboo.

On the street of a thousand
sighs in Hanoi
I found a simple Buddha
high on a gold lacquered shelf
in a small room of the honored dead.

Pulled down to my knees
by a girl in a yellow ao dai,
I was no longer afraid
of the spirit I was
trying to become the man.

ii

Before me, my father's
immigrant father
appeared in rosy incense smoke.

He who had made shoes from sheets of hard leather
with his hands and a knife.

He who had fixed all broken things
and butchered lambs in spring.
He who in his anger
had made my father kneel on dry corn
his raging hands had shucked
across the bathroom floor.

iii

I have never knelt on dry corn,
the way my father
has never prayed
on the floor of a stranger's
house in Hanoi,

yet through the years
that cling
to the razor sharp kernels

came the belt
and the backhands
out of nowhere, my father,
beating like an angel
for heaven, through me.

Words for the Husky Girl

I see her pretty bulk there
in the summer drunken days.
Her mother dressed her
like a princess
so the bows and rows
of white and pink chiffon
would make her seem as thin and light
as air that raised her skirts.

Our sins are great.
We taunted her like hungry
wild dogs at flesh fresh torn
and trembling in high grass.
Our sins are great.
Our dreadful hunger fades.

At the Dreamland Theater, 1959

Flash of your sex, Mr.,
           then the boy's white face
drained of blood, and his eyes

rolled back into his head.
           You of the hands in your pockets.
You of the heart that beat dead.

I thought someday I'd understand.
           You of the shuffling feet.
You of the back of the bus.

You of the end of our longing
           who grabbed the boy whom no one loved
and so like you

came every week alone,
           and held him wriggling on the dark
and sticky floor, and took

before you could be stopped
           a small flame from inside him
and crushed it out with your hands.

You of the blue alone,
           you of the vacant eyes,
you of the cave in your chest, we remember.

That Finished Feeling

Wrong words brought them together
       outside the steel mill
bar of tired, nervous men,

wrong words to the wrong man,
       wrong street, wrong night
the blood so near their skin

that this man full of iron ingot's
       heat, and this other good man
in their rage

crossed a line
       which in the August
night is pure

so they face off,
       and in our muted needs
we circle their sweat-shined

muscle and bone
       twisted in the light
of the night shift cranes

beating   beating
    Oh say can you see
these strong and grown men

whose lives are too heavy
    to bear the bloody other
stranger into another day.

Hanoi, Christmas 1992

The small strange dog rubs his raw back
against the crude table's leg

exposing more and more raw flesh to the sun.
Flea-infested and mangy, he loves no one

but the old man who sits in the banyan's shade
watching evening overcome us,

his wispy beard
lifting in the breeze

like leaves of the areca.
Slowly, from a deep well,

another man pulls water.
To save myself from this dog

I take refuge
in the face of a small girl

who plays with dirty feet
all around the house of the old poet

we have come to pay our homage to
beyond the temple of this lake. Lost

in her beauty, I was soothed,
though I still felt the world

tilt, as if on the edge of a plate.
One small patch of bamboo. One deep well.

One house with a high place to sleep.
One tree of the five-star fruit. One life.

Hymn of My Republic

Summer of my dumb awakening,
nineteen fifty-six, a solitary

neighbor man who walked every day to the mill
through south Lorain with a gimpy stride

and lived alone above the bar of our fathers
emerged into light

and passed around among us boys
who chanced to be nearby

and not afraid
some cool gear

from his war,
number WW II.

I got the leather pilot's hat, oh lord.
I put it on

and nothing could touch me
wandering long into the dusk,

hymn of my republic
on my lips, my rough spirit

raised up somehow into glory, that boy's
grave initiative,

that blood
spilled first in the roses.

Cleaning out the Shaker Gears, Elyria Foundry, Elyria, Ohio, 1971

I'd done my year in the green place
where I'd found myself
in a dark hole or two, in the ground,
among machines that could crush your skull,
though this is before I'd read Dante.
New on the job so they sent me
down into the hole, below the huge
shaker that broke loose black sand
from castings of diesel engine motor blocks
big as whales,
beautiful things like you might
dream in a dream of order
in a world that otherwise
spits hot metal into your face.
Ten steps down I found the tunnel.
I found the first dim red light
and crawled into the first room of gears
that were quiet now
but that seemed to shimmer
or seemed somehow about to move.
I did not want to be among them,
to step between them
to sweep black sand
and chipped gray iron away,
but I crawled to the red light
visible through black air
like a ship's light,
to the next room of gears.

Above me,
the hate of no reason
was born in the imaginations
of the heavy bodied
dark souled men
who'd plotted briefly
then blasted
the silence of my tunnel
with the sudden sharp
whine of gear motors kicking in,
shattering my ears in the instant
I'd lifted my legs away.
How did they know.

From the House on Nguyen Du

One pile of squid
stretched on small bamboo kites
drying in the sun

One driver asleep near his cyclo
in the shade of banyans
by the lake of the returned sword

One wild dog
chasing rats into the sewer
his head like a fox

His tail like the rat's
he does not speak my tongue
my smell is foreign to him

One pile of gladiolus
pink and white
in the cyclo's empty seat

Waiting to be taken to the lover
who tends her misery
in the city's ancient heart

One street of paper shoes
and votive paper
clothes for the dead

One ball of fire
hurling itself into my face
in the first dream in-country

One long fever that took me
so far up heaven's ladder
I was surrounded

By two men, and a boy
lovely as the Buddha
in failing light

One set of needles
twisted and tapped
into the meridian

Of nerves in my back and arms
one set of joss sticks
white hot as charcoal

Held by the men and the boy
to the bridges of my blood
until my heart is warmed

One scream
when the nerve of sickness
is finally tapped

One hour of sweat and delusion
until the small reed boat
piled with lotus blossoms

Sails a wide circle
out and away
that signifies the world

Our 17th Street Years

Just the luck of the draw

my father would say

slouched in his white T-shirt

longneck bottle of beer

dangling from his terrible hand

He'd meant to tell me what the world was

so I imagined

a life of my hand held out

the good spirits waiting somehow

in the misty bamboo groves   yet

no words came as I had hoped

no webs of light connecting me

no paths that said to follow

no dove against the sky   no sky

Carp

We fished for carp whose flesh would never find
our lips, the bottom feeders fathers said to kill.
We fished at night with bloody bait designed
to draw them up from river mud. Our will
was to possess a life not ours, to make
those glowing spirit bodies understand
our need for blood spilled simply for the sake
of what we thought it took to be a man.
I'll never understand that rage we knew,
that knife that someone gouged into the eyes
of carp we caught but didn't think to do
the killing right, and wasted lives despised
for reasons lost now in the blur of days.
Not boys, but something darker, something crazed.

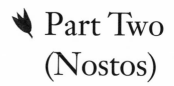 # Part Two
(Nostos)

Then one of the seraphs
flew to me with a live coal
in his hand, which he had
taken from the altar. With
it he touched my
mouth and said, "See, this
has touched your lips; your
guilt is taken away and
your sin atoned for."
—Isaiah 6:6

Conversation of Our Blood

That his father brought the butcher up
to tattoo a watch in indigo
on my grandfather's wrist
with the time his steerage
would unbound its lines
and sail,
not for a new world,
just a different one,
is as true as this sky I could love.
But please, only you
of continents abandoned
pass judgment,
only you of quarantine
and the various cleansings
and the dialects
impossible to understand.

His mother wrapped some bread up
in a white square of light
and from their stone house on the hill
they must have walked
north to the station
across the pasture
and followed the tracks
in what must have seemed
a moment outside the world,
the gray dawn coming down
on their sweet and level plain.
From the station they traveled

further north
in a crowded common car
that must have lulled them to the harbor
and the great pushing
mass of men like him,
and their women
dragging children through the mud
and the green confusion,
his father not stopping
to wave from the dock,
his wrist burning the blue time.

By the fish smell and oil drum din
he bedded down
something in my chest tells me.
With his blanket
I imagine him mark out his place.
I rub my face
to try and find
the shape of his jaw
and I do, and his love for the good drink
which is never the last,
and the startled look of surprise
always in our eyes
and the pull of him,
like a wire, in my heart.

The years that I didn't know mattered
must have been those
black wings that passed through us
and were gone.
I finally took the slow,

heaving ferry out
to where you waited
your long Ellis Island hours.
I tried to find a column
you would have leaned against,
a window out of which
you would have seen your world
taking shape
across the river we stole, Grandfather,
as we stole all our rivers.

Seeking the Redwing

Seeking the redwing
on the lonely river

no fish rising
no hatch on the wing

yet so much wide and willing
light invades this valley

you may be blessed.
In the willow bends,

waist deep in the quick cold
you may be delivered

to a dream or a prayer.
(Some have been taken clean away.)

Seeking the redwing
inside the brain

where the you assembled
stitch by stitch

by the precious family grief,
the ordinary grief,

yearns to be water
cut through the limestone way.

Three Fish

Duc Thanh brought me three fish
      he had caught in the small lake on Nguyen Du.

They were the color of pearls;
      they were delicate and thin. Already

winter was in the wind from China,
      voices of ancestors on swan's wings.

This late in the season,
      evening traffic's hum and weave beginning to rise

beyond the guardians of the gate,
      these fish are a great gift.

I was in my room,
      lost in a foreign silence.

I wanted to eat the miles up somehow,
      I wanted to split my soul in two

so I could stay forever
      in the musty guest house pleasures.

I was that far away, that lost
      when he called to me, ghost that he is,

across the courtyard, and in moonlight,
      held up three silver fish.

Our Middle Years

Because in our middle years
        we had grown contemplative,
we asked out loud for the fire;

we had grown mostly cautious too,
        except in matters of the flesh
between the thighs.

We were waiting out the end of the century
        and wondered where the fire had gone,
night sky

empty as a skirt
        except for the wing bone noise
of the night hawk

diving for insects
        with a more than abundant precision
required by our times.

Brother Crow of Pearl Avenue

Madame X kept a crow
whose tongue she had split

with a razor to make it talk.
Its wings were my blue desire;

its beak black and pointed in perfection.
I love you she'd say into his face

and then hold him into splendor,
into sunlight on her arm

where he spoke to us
in a voice that sounded

lost inside the hollow bones,
so I thought This must be the world opening,

how the spirit doesn't die
but takes the shape of crows

whose tongues are split to make them talk,
and what I tried to grab onto,

digging with my nails into its flesh,
was a holy life.

When the Hunger Is Gone

The sky is pink,
the morning should be clear and cool
and not this canopy of heat and muggy air,
and where you are tonight you see the many ghosts,
and though they long to find their homes,
the most they'll ever have again
are strangers driving through their wind-cut
rocky caves, the few who feel a ripple through their nerves
and sing out loud as if their song
could make them new again.
It cannot make them new.
How wrong I was to think there was a healing way
to travel through the dark.

But long for someone in another's house,
and the day may take a wild turn or two;
you could believe a lover's hand
was reaching through the hazy summer air
no matter what the thieves of hearts
have practiced more than once inside the body
that you were those nights you opened up.
I opened up for you that way.

I thought that I would never get enough.
Your hands were deep inside of me,
our thrashing rough
and witnessed only by the sticky rain,
your lips still burning where you found the skin
that no one cared to find before.

You gave your patient hands, my wife,
to soothe what's been undone in me
so long I thought that I was meant to pay and pay.
The gun is always never in my hands;
the blood we spilled
unreal except the salty taste against my lips,
that boy I'd tried to breathe alive.

I want to stop the stinging, burning bees
inside this hive of days.

Rhapsody

On Broadway down in south Lorain
three street kids rap the evening into place

their music like the biting wind
that lashes this bodega's waste

their songs are frozen on their breath
like ghosts they rise around our heads

they riff and glide and love to feel
the words take shape

The Here and the There

As one house moved nearer death
(though the corn was high and tasseled)
the other grew more fierce in its living.
Forgive us, Ruth,
the ache that came in waves.
We had a certain hunger to go back,
but Sunday no breeze came to the willow,
no ringing in the empty house.

I saw you lift your hand in lamplight,
someone came for you.
I felt you in my room,
your sudden sharp good-bye
a rapture gone.

On Mai Hac De, *Anniversary of the Liberation*

Women from the country carry baskets
        at the ends of long balanced sticks,
sometimes on top of their heads,

and move slowly through the city
        calling out in a song
the names of the foods they sell.

In lovely receding degrees
        their songs fade as they pass
down this street, then it's gone

until a high note rises
        above the traffic noise
and it comes again

to fade away at last
        as the fearful, lonely dogs
begin their evening howl

to be let inside, with the others.
        Twenty years since the tanks
rolled through the gates of the palace.

Elegy for Peter

That night we drank warm whiskey
in our parked car
beyond woods now lost to the suburbs,
I fell in love with you.

What waited was the war
like a bloody curtain,
and a righteous moment
when the lovely boy's

spine was snapped,
then the long falling into hell.
But lately, you've been calling me
back through the years of bitter silence

to tell me of another river of blood
and of the highland's
howl at dusk of human voices
blasted into ecstasy.

That night in sweet Lorain
we drank so long and hard
we raised ourselves
above the broken places,

mill fires burning
red against the sky. Why
is there is no end
to this unraveling.

My Early Training

On the banks of West Lake near Hanoi
  the Abbot stepped from shadows
at Tran Quoc Pagoda. Wind

lifted lotus blossoms;
  spirits released themselves
from banyan roots old as Christ.

The holy man pointed my way
  towards two skinny dogs
playing like children in the perfumed garden

and then to the Buddha, high on an altar
  beyond the dusty, sun-reeked
courtyard of my imaginings, a lesson

I still struggle to understand.
  And oh the days and ways of woe since then,
this moon who won't love us

as we need, only the unrequited touch,
  only the empty skin on skin of stolen hours
fractured out of time

and these sharp wings that beat
  through black, star-shredded space
vast as memory, but not everlasting.

Meditation at Melville Ave.

I'd fallen asleep
on the white wicker chair
on the back porch,
the green yard and garden
so lush it seemed almost
as if the hot, troubled city
was not pressing in
against every inch of air.
Hot for so early in June
yet a breeze came now and then
to shake the live oak's branches
and turn the maple's leaves
up as if a storm were near.
I'd fallen asleep and dreamed
I was someone else,
someone wholly unburdened
and with hope.
I had been briefly among friends
who had gone away to a wedding
of other friends
who were also strangers,
only the green war between us,
only the sandalwood smell in her hair.
Half in and out of sleep
I heard two sets of chimes
in wind that came and went
and seemed to play a song
that rose and fell,
some form my body knew.

Beyond the yard,
sirens played out their flat complaint.
Trouble. He got drunk.
She spit in his face.
He lashed out at her.
If you think there's no blood
in the streets
then you live in a dream.
The chimes rose and fell
and rose and fell again.
The friends stay and stay.
The witnesses of evening
all settle into the cacophony
of familiar fears.
The silver leaves turn up
but no storm comes.

For the Novice of Tran Quoc Pagoda

She says she knows what the dead say to the living,
that they remember us from time to time.
For her, that place is real, and is forgiving,
and not a world without dimension, but kind
in most unhuman ways,
with space enough
for all the spirits lost to touch,
in need of union, sometimes of love.
She doesn't think that there's a river
still or deep as need to carry souls across,
or paths that mark our way.
She says the dead are lashed
to nothingness, like blood
spilled on our living hands.

Meditation in Hue

Some nights I still fear the dark among trees,
those last few ambush hours before morning.

I fear the jungle of a thousand sighs
which calls and calls to me.

I don't care I have to tell you
about the angels who fell

dead from gun ships into the valley of tears.
I don't care if I keep you from the wedding wine.

Priests blessed weapons in the mist of Ca Lu.
I want to die in the mango groves

of this green river valley,
children dancing after my corpse.

First Letter to Calumpang

But I recall
your eyes burned into me,
desire inside the inn unleashed.
There is a blood from touching, and a fire;
I've had them in my mouth.
I've known the most amazing hours with you.
Long afternoons of slow entangled
drowsing in the heat.
The muslin slip your mother chose
that called and called my hands to you.
We tied our tongues inside our mouths
then rose, our blood in step,
at last our wayward spirits home.
Your hand held once again, then gone.

Chain

Three crows squawk madly in noon heat
　　　below the river
dried to a slip

of brackish water
　　　in the locks
and though there's no

confirmation,
　　　their pure announcements
are just enough

to turn your long stride
　　　away from the small time
excursion

into someone else's
　　　practiced moves,
Oh field of sheets.

Crows so vivid
　　　must mean something
in a day otherwise

lost to the endless bickering,
          the many small indignities.
What ground you think you stand on,

depends upon
          what ground you haunt
with your desires.

On the Ambiguity of Injury and Pain

When I saw the X ray of my boy's broken bones
the young doctor held up to the light,
a fist closed around my heart.
Behind us in the gurney
he was lost in his pain,
betrayed by the world
like birds by false spring.
The little Mozart piece would be abandoned
to summer evenings jangled out of time,

and back at school
his classmates rush to him
in wonder at his wound
and scratch their names into the plaster.
And tonight, when I bathe him he is shy.
When I try to run the soap
and rag between his legs
he stops me with his free hand
the way I've been stopped by women.
We move in the old way, around each other.
Kisses so sweet. Dark room of joy.

Red Squirrel

I think it's fine the squirrel lives with us,
in secret in our fifties-style ranch
beneath the pale, unsheltered sky.
From the world she is a gift of sorts,
a strange and awkward blessing
who wakes us from our cold dawn sleep

to watch the sun come up through trees.
I think it means the air in here must be alive;
the stale basement walls a womb,
a nest inside a womb beyond
the muted rise and fall, our voices
as we move from room to room.

And she must know the odd forgiven terrors
of the family life, the love that has to fight
to stay alive. So from this man at my front door
I turn away, his traps and poison
held before him like a gift, a gilded
reckless sin I know for once not to embrace.

Meditation at La Grange

Fields unroll in my brain
towards a green center.

Because we are sad we injure the earth
We injure the earth because we are sad.

A boy broke out of me once,
and ran wild

between furrows fresh turned,
and he could kill or love

the blinding slats of light
cut through the god damned

branches of the dying elms,
and he could kill or love the lark.

Words Like Cold Whiskey between Us and Pain

I no longer covet the stranger's wife.
He had opened his house to me

one night when I didn't know
what world I was in.

We had only the green war in common,
the Jacob's ladder to climb.

We were deep in the country,
evening coming down like a gate,

all the good creatures stirred into song
when she came outside after dishes

and stood in the backdrop kitchen light,
her hair matted black at her temples

and her eyes
lit in the satisfaction

of good work done
and in my mind I wanted her,

my face a shameless
mask in the dark.

I thought I could smell the river.
I thought I could hear its rush.

Stars began to beat down on us.
It doesn't mean anything. Here, I let you go.

The Veil Lifted

Moon in its skin,
        arms where nothing gathers,
sky that could open like lips.

I wanted to tell you of the voices
        I heard. Too small yet for school,
my father in the fiery mill,

my mother in a cold meat locker,
        I wandered the streets, sun-blasted
by false spring and heard

the dogs start up, and birds
        flutter the nervous leaves
and locusts clack and chirr

until a silence fell.
        No one in sight when the sun
slid away and the sky opened black,

and a woman walked out of the trees
        who spoke to me in tongues;
radiant and strange,

she'd come up with the carnival
        of cheap rides
that pitched its tents

in the park near the river's song.
　　　Where the fathers in white T-shirts,
pockets full of change,

oh la, would stride in the dusk
　　　to the sideshow rubber lady
and the frog boy no one could love.

We had not yet lost the spirit
　　　of sugar spun in webs
like ancient hair, the tilt-o-whirl,

the hawker's eyes
　　　I couldn't turn away.
Yes to the frog boy

anxious for home.
　　　Yes to the rubber lady, bless
what she did with her legs in the air.

Only the mad need apply.
　　　Only the spirits
called into living

reckless with longing,
　　　with love when it eats you,
veil lifted at last.

Bear Meadow

In this field of day lilies
just opening, beating for sun
in this lush summer bear meadow,
I tried to find a way
to stay in your world, wife.
The field hummed with life,
the bugs and frogs
and jeering birds
but no words came
as I had hoped
from the sky
blue as a marble.
I tried to lose my self
in the woods of beyond
but only paths fell under my feet
and I glimpsed the shape
that nature is
unfolding in the roots
and limbs connecting us
with threads of light
but then so quickly gone.
I could imagine
an emptiness without you,
without your face in my hands
like a flower
I could imagine something
bottomless and cold.
We have traveled
deep into the center

of something we can't name
yet stayed side by side
when the light died
and the road ground down
to a cutback through trees
and there was nowhere to run.
What I have to give you
I feel in my blood,
many small fires
burning into one.

Fever Dream in Hanoi

The gold red and green carp
surfaces in the lake where I struggle.
Angry and impatient with me
he shakes his head
big as a baby's head
towards the lake's center.
I'd been half-swimming,
half-treading water
to try to make the shore
where small lights
blinked around the perimeter
beside tiny stands
where women squat
in that particular
Vietnamese way
selling their few packs of cigarettes,
their few bottles of warm beer.

Lovers linger too,
among banyan trees tangled.
They nuzzle each other.
They coo and laugh
for the minutes stolen
from the crowded family houses,
and all seem to call to me
when I wake in the lake
of the returned sword
to the carp who shakes his head

towards the shrine on the island
lit only with light
of the Buddha's eyes.

I thought my life was calling
from the lamp-lit lovers' shore.
I thought my death called too
from the dark water, deeper,
but the carp shakes his head,
old hooks and fishing line
strung in the moon like a beard.
He swishes the fan of his tail
and I'm on my back,
floating somehow towards the temple,
face of the carp
changed, a human smile
on his lips, the moon
slashed across the blood-gills' pulse.
The lovers turn away from each other
to the lake's black edge,
and the old women
blow out their small lanterns
and turn too towards the lake.
I'm being towed now,
the gold carp's hooks
snagged through the skin on my back.
With his eyes he tells me
not to fight.
He tells me of my perfect death
waiting at the shrine
and then I wake,
burning with fever

in the guest house on Nguyen Du
by the lake where lovers
walk in the dark
evening's desire.
Two men and a boy

hold coal-hot doss sticks
to points on my wrists and feet
where my cold blood is still.
Another man taps needles
deep into my back
down my spine
until a cry or grunt
escapes my lips
and he nods
his happy affirmation
as my gut begins to stir,
a snake coming alive,
uncurling itself inside me,
my head swimming,
my skin hot then cold
then hot again,
musty waves of sickness
through which he tows me
with his needles
and I float.
I let go of everything.
I let go my family
the thousands of miles away.
I let go my days
and my hours
and my sad minutes

and I let go the love
of those in whose minds
I let go the words.
Every word ever uttered.
I let go the world.
I spin off the world,
hooks in my back
pulling me upwards, upwards and away.

Notes

The lines "¡Con la belleza no se come! / ¿Qué piensas que en la vida?" (You cannot eat the beauty! / What do you think life is?) are from Angel Gonzalez, *Astonishing World*, translated by Steven Ford Brown and Gutierrez Revuelta (Milkweed, 1993).

"Hanoi, Christmas 1992" is for Pham Tien Duat.

"Conversation of Our Blood" is in memory of Ivan Grasa, 1896–1975.

"Three Fish" is in memory of Ngo Vinh Vien.

"The Here and the There" is written in memory of Ruth Weigl.

"Elegy for Peter" is in memory of Peter J. Shagovac, killed outside Da Nang, 1967.

"Meditation at Melville Ave." is for Leslie and Kevin.

"On Mai Hac De, Anniversary of the Liberation" is for Huu Thinh, who assigned this poem in Hanoi.

"On the Ambiguity of Injury and Pain" is for Andrew Weigl, and is published here with his permission.

"Red Squirrel" is for Dave Smith.

"Bear Meadow" is for J.K.W.

"Fever Dream in Hanoi" is for B.H.